Poems Volume I

Chloe Masters

Chloe Masters

POEMS VOLUME I

To Connor
You make my life brighter than it ever has been

It may seem foolish to admit
But I find myself drowning
In only the idea of you and me

The fear of you realizing how much of a burden
The act of loving me can be
It keeps me awake at night

But the thought of you accepting it
Accepting every broken and breaking part of me
That is what lulls me to sleep

I need you
Not in the ways to survive
But in the ways that make life worth living

If there is some way I can convince you to stay
I wouldn't hesitate
I would spin my words into the most beautiful tapestry

This version of existence is cruel at times
But there is an underlying beauty of it all

The way you smile
The way you look at me
The way you say my name
The way your hand fits in mine

The beauty of you
The beauty of us
There is nothing more beautiful

I wish I could confess that I love you again
Now I have the words
Now I have the feelings

Now I know what loving you feels like
It's suffocating and breathing

It's the first breath of air after drowning
It's coming in from the cold
It's stepping into the ocean after years of missing it

Loving you is peace
It's hope
It's euphoria
It's everything I've been missing coming back

Loving you is looking forward to the future
One where I'm yours
And you're mine

There are things I never want to stop
Things that I would die to keep
Things I would beg on my knees for

The first thing is the way you look at me
When your eyes light up with stars
When your smile creates lines outside your eyes

The second is the way you hold me
When your arms wrap around my waist to pull me close
When you squeeze me tightly

Third, but not last
When you listen to my rambles
Like you could hear me talk for hours

It's strange
To dream of you even when I'm wide awake

I can see a cottage in the woods
Baked bread and home-cooked meals
Hidden figures painted in the cupboards
Tucked in the crevices of the house

I dream of seeing far-off places
Our hands gripping each other
As our feet take us to see things we haven't seen
The experience made better because we're together

I can see adventures
I can see peaceful nights under the stars
I can see us sitting and laughing together
I can see us

There's magic to it
The way you found parts of me I forgot existed
Parts that I lost a long time ago

With you, I found a special kind of love
A love I no longer thought was real
A love I'd stopped believing in

I'm excited to live it out
The love you've made me believe
The love of small gestures
The love of quiet mornings

I'm grateful for it
Your love when I only knew heartache
Your love when I was at my worst
Your love when I couldn't breath

Sometimes it feels as though I've lived in two worlds
One with you
And one without

The one without you
It was terrifying
I was alone and scared
I couldn't trust my own thoughts

This new one
The one with you
It's a haven
I'm safe and cared for

The other world is still a part of me
I remember it occasionally
But the memories that come
Are no match for the new ones we've made

Your hand constantly searches
I didn't know what it was looking for at first

But when our fingers, at last, twisted together
I understood
And I squeezed you tight

Then your other hand wrapped around my waist
And my heart thundered so loud I feared you
could hear it

Then your head found its way to my chest
And I almost cried

It was more perfect than anything else
And I found myself imagining falling asleep in
your arms

It breaks my heart
When you feel the need to say
You don't know why I'm in love with you

I'm in love with you because I only need a minute
To find a thousand things that I love about you

I'm in love with you because you listen
I know I'll never receive judgment for my words

I'm in love with you because I know you'll always be there
I know if I ever need safety I'll find it in your arms

I'm in love with you for a never-ending amount of reasons
And I could fill a thousand pages with I'm in love with you

Truth be told I wasn't looking when I found you
And I was content calling you my friend

Truth be told I wasn't expecting it
The way I fell for you
Plummeting headfirst

Truth be told I was scared to tell you
Scared it would ruin our friendship

Truth be told I was shocked
When you told me you felt the same

Truth be told I fear losing you
Because I don't think I could live without you

When will you realize that I don't want anyone else
You're the only one that I want to spend my life with

When will you realize
That the idea of waking up next to you is what keeps me happy

When will you realize
That seeing the world with you sounds like paradise

When will you realize
I would do anything to let you know that I love you

The story of Icarus never seemed cautionary
He loved the sun enough to risk it all

I would risk it
Everything around me
Just for the chance of getting to love you

Icarus flew toward the sun
Because his heart wanted to feel his embrace
He was desperate for it

He knew the cost
Just like I did
I knew it would kill me if you melted my wings

Despite the ocean below
I still raced for your arms
And how shocking it was when you pulled me close

Sometimes the weight of loneliness crushes me beyond reason
It crushes my joints and my ribs
It clamps its hands over my ears and mouth
It squeezes the air from my lungs and the blood from my heart

It tortures me until I can't do anything other than sob
I wonder what I could do to ease it
To pull its grasp from my body
The only solution seems just out of reach

My own mistakes and inaction brought me here
I am now at its mercy
This beast that now sits on my chest
Right where I imagined your head to be

If loving you could be a sin
Then by God, I'll be the biggest sinner
I would abandon redemption
I would abandon all hope for my soul

There would be no need to be dragged
I would walk hand-in-hand with the Devil
I would dive into the pits of hell myself
If only to have a chance with you

I believe there's something holy about it
Being in love with you
If there's Heaven on Earth
Then it's wherever you are

I imagine you taste like brandy
I get hopelessly drunk on your kiss
I imagine you smell like wood smoke
Smothering my mind with nothing but your existence

You have the same effect as summer campfires
As late nights in a lake
As mason jars of moonshine

I can feel your arms around me
Even if you're miles away

You found me on the steps of the church
Its walls no longer offer sanctuary
Its priest stood in his steeple perch
Your extended hand made me wary

How do you abandon it?
The only thing you know to be true
But when it deems your nature unfit
You will be dragged by your neck from the pew

The priest will ignore your desperation
He will cut your knees on the pavement
He will scream about your damnation
He will claim you are an ailment

You found me on the steps of the church
You offered me a chance in a real sanctuary
The priest still watched from his steeple perch
Your outstretched hand no longer made me wary

The weight of being responsible
For yourself, for others
There comes a time when it breaks you
And I'm wondering if I'm living through a breaking point

My tongue no longer cares if the words it spews sting
They are sharp and truthful
It has lived a life of pretty lies
And it tires of falsehoods

My mind no longer cares about carrying the grievances of others
They get dropped if they get too heavy
It has lived a life of being less important
And it tires of second place

My body has taken every one of your punches
And my hands are finally ready to fight back

Was it worth it?
Years of hate disguised as love
Because you really do hate
You hate everything I've become without you

I pulled away from your life
And created a life of my own
It's better, safer, and entirely, purely me
There is not a speck of you in it

Was it worth it?
Knowing that death is coming for you
And when it grabs you
I will not be paying respects

Are you ready for it?
I've seen my afterlife
It's the opposite of what you've said

Maybe you were just describing yours
There is anger and then there is grief
Both are essential to life
Both represent pain
Both can tear down cities

Anger is harsh, cruel
Like a sharp blade cutting through
It leaves blood in its wake
It leaves scars on people

Greif is also cruel
But it's cruel like a broken bone
It takes months to heal
Sometimes it never does

Angry grief is something else entirely
It loosens tongues, makes them spiteful
It opens the mind to more and more pain
It is the cruellest, it hurts the most

I don't understand why I'm grieving
All I know is that it hurts
It's pushing my shoulders in
It's making my steps heavy

There is an unexplained weight in my chest
I hate everything you stand for
So why is your pain affecting me
Why is your disaster making me crumble

I'm tired of worrying about you
Get out of my head
Get out of my heart
Leave me alone

I don't understand why I feel like this
I am drowning in grief
I am in pain
I am in pain and you are once again the cause

I doubt I am deserving of any form of your affection
I know my own body
I know my own mind
And they are my worst enemies

You don't deserve someone with a failing body
You don't deserve to see the day-in, day-out pain

It isn't pretty
The days I can't get out of bed
The nights I spend tossing and turning
Tearing through sheets and pillows

I am unsure about a lot of things
About my head, about my body
But I am sure of my heart's desire
And it is longing for your affection

Wanderlust is the most human emotion
We are constantly searching for some new adventure
Something we haven't seen
Anything new to quench our thirst

Lakes discovered and yet untouched
Mountains unclimbed by our legs
Winds that haven't blown past our faces

A new friend, whose story we don't know
Whose laugh we haven't memorized

A new lover, whose kiss we haven't felt
Whose hands have not traced our skin

I know some strange words
Knowing them pulls away the cloth over my heart
I know some strange emotions

There's a word I know
Mornden
It's the word used to describe what happens to two people over a long weekend
Where they leave the world alone and let the days last forever

Querinous is another one
The longing to know whether someone is who you're going to wake up with for twenty thousand mornings
So you can stop counting them one-by-one

The last one is immerensis
It describes the feeling of knowing you have problems and require daily care to function
But no matter how guilty you feel
The person you love is so eager to help

I haven't had you long
Calling you mine is a new experience
But I already can't imagine life without you

I'll roll into my pillows when you're not there
The smell of you lingers for days
It's a comfort I didn't know I needed

I'll trace the spots I remember you kissing
The feeling of you lingers for days

It's nearly maddening
The way we can be apart but you're still so close

I know you said to take things slow
But some of the words you say
Make me question whether you'd rather move fast

You talk about the future
You use the words "our" and "we"

You talk about our wedding
Our home
Our lives

You talk about travelling
We go together
We share the world

You talk about the future
And it's like all that matters is that we do it together

People will claim their favourite season is the one made for lovers
I'm here to tell you every season is for love

Winter is cold mornings spent curled in bed a little longer
It's for hot chocolate with your beloved
It's for shared blankets and kisses to keep warm

Spring is planting gardens together
It's for clearing the brush left over from the year before
It's for finding the perfect spot for a picnic

Summer is spending late nights together
It's for adventures with hands intertwined
It's for falling asleep under the stars together

Autumn is for baking apple pie together
It's for visiting fall festivals and getting lost in corn mazes
It's for picking pumpkins and carving them in the kitchen together

I've always been surrounded by love
Even if most of the time
It wasn't love meant for me

Sometimes observation is the best way to learn
I've seen love persevere
I've seen it survive the worst of life's challenges
I've seen it come out stronger than before

I believe this love we share can do that
I want to see how far we can go

I want to know the love I've grown up watching
And I want it to be meant for me

It takes time for me to really know what you say
My mind needs time to weed through the words

It can take minutes
Hours
Days

No matter how long it takes
The hidden meaning always dawns on me
What you were really saying always reveals itself

I enjoy the puzzles you leave
Buried in casual sentences

Do you mean to do it?
Distract me from my day-to-day tasks
I can't help but stop and think of you

Your never-ending questions that turn into hour-long conversations
The way every time you discover something new about me it ends with a kiss
Each time I brush my hair from my face I imagine it's you
The lingering feeling of your hand on my waist lasts for days

Even though you step out of my door
You never truly leave me

I want to be loved
I want someone to look at me and see me
I long to be someone to someone

The back of my hand longs to be kissed
My lifeline wants a kind finger to trace it

I have scars and moles that need to be kissed
My imperfections long to be perfect
My body longs to be treasured
My heart longs to be held the same way it's held by others

I long to feel love the same way it's described in books
I want someone to read my entire soul
I long for a love that is devotion
That is reverence
I long to be someone to someone

There are two constants to humanity
Art and War
Art has always existed
War has always existed

Art envelopes our hands
The hands of painters, inventors, writers
Everything that is touched is art
Everyone that breathes is an artist

War envelopes our hearts
The hearts of lovers, parents, children
Everything that is touched is war
Everyone that breathes is a soldier

I miss the ocean
The sound of it crashing on the beach
Matching my own footfalls as I run to it
Like it misses me the same way

I kick off my shoes as I run
Running faster than I ever have
Running until I hit the water

Running until I pause

Waves crash against my legs
The wind blows my hair from my face
The sun warms my skin

When the waves retreat
My feet follow them

I walk until I cannot feel the sand beneath me
Then I let the water take me

And I am floating
And I am free

I hate the saying
"I'd die for you"

Ending the one guarantee on this planet
Ending your life
Just to prove your devotion

Living for someone isn't good either
Having one person be the reason you stay alive
It's dangerous

So I will not die for you
I will not live for you

I will live for me
So we may live together

My first name has a meaning
It means blooming
Like a flower in spring
Like potential

My second name has a meaning
It means beautiful
Like a lover's smile
Like opportunity

My third name has a meaning
It means gift of the sea
Like the sound of waves on a beach
Like freedom

Despite this
Despite my name meaning I am a gift from the sea
I could not be farther from her waters

There are times when I forget what I've lived through
When I have gotten so used to the trauma
They seem secondary to everything else

But you're always asking questions
And I'm always giving answers

I'll talk about something I've been through
And I'll say it so casually
But you'll always look at me the same

You always pull me closer
You always kiss my head
You always apologize for something that isn't your fault

I'd ask why
But I think I know
You can feel the pain I felt so long ago

Sometimes I'll just stare at a piece of paper for hours

My hands need to write
They thirst to make words on a page
They long to fly over the paper

However, my mind hinders them
It lacks ideas
Inspiration
Energy

I always want to write
Sometimes I just don't know what

I always long to be somewhere else
Somewhere in the future

When it's cold I long to be on a farm
Throwing wood onto a fire
A new baked good in the oven
Waiting for my loved ones to join me in the house I built

In the heat, I long to be in a new place
Seeing things I haven't seen
Eating food I haven't tasted
Laughing with friends over a good drink

I'm always waiting for the day I wake up in my lover's arms
Knowing I have the rest of my life to wake up that way
I'm always waiting for the rest of my life

Every time I wake up in your arms
I think of waking up in them for the rest of my life
I imagine your hand in my hair even in sleep
Your breathing is something I have memorized

When we eat together
I think of sitting down for dinner
Or your arm around my waist while I put food on our plates

I think about you coming home to the house we share
I think about something as simple as grocery shopping
I think about sharing lazy morning kisses to start the day

I imagine our future
A future we share

I sometimes wonder why you love my storm
Why do you pick my thunder
My lightning
My rain

There are clearer skies out there
Bright blue with warm suns

But you chose an ancient storm
One that's been raging for years
One that shows no sign of calming

It is not a storm I want you to sail on
And yet you tie yourself to the mast and send your ship into it
You do not fear its waves

I might be a poet
I might be able to spin words the way a painter mixes their medium
But every painter needs a subject
And every poet needs a muse

My muse can be grief
More often than not it is anger
Those poems are the ones I needed to write
Poems that came bursting out of me
Loud and raging

Recently you've become every poem I've written
You are hidden behind every word
You are the reason behind the feelings

So, I may be a poet
But you will always be the words

You ask me why I keep my nails long
Why do I care so much about them

It's because they are the closest thing I have to claws
They are the one thing I've always had
So I keep them sharp and ready

Once upon a time, I was without them
People insisted I be declawed

Once upon a time, I needed them
Their absence meant pain

But those who told me to cut them
They left me defenceless
I will not be hurt again

I know it would never be you
But I'm still afraid of getting hurt

Ages ago
Two women died together
A boat was built for them

Ancient stories
Could they have been ancient lovers?

The boat was carried to a hill
Horses, ox, and dogs are buried with them
Two women are buried together

Their burial is now a major artifact
Their deaths transcend generations

I have been hiding under anger for too long
Anger is sharp, it's coarse
It grinds down your mind until you are too exhausted to do anything

Sometimes it sticks to your bones
Dragging you down until the only thing you feel is pain
It's exhausting to be angry

I am tired

Tired of anger
Tired of rage

Tired of never knowing anything besides varying levels of anger

Female rage isn't just anger
It is generations of wrongs
It is years of pain
Years of silent endurance

Rage isn't the right word
Neither is fury
It's something more
Something stronger

Female rage is knowing you should have every right
To seize every opportunity
To get retribution for the things done to you and your sisters

But you're forced to wait
Stuck waiting for karma
Stuck waiting for the glory of payback

I think I forgot that after the anger
There should be healing
The damage that caused the anger needs to be repaired
I have yet to heal years-old damage

I'm finally experiencing healing
But the scars of anger still remain

Can you heal them?
Can you accept the scars even if you can't mend
Can you hold my hand while I bear them?

Even with all the time in the world
There is not enough of it
I need endless hours to sort through my mind

Sometimes there is nothing but a knot of words
Twisted and tight

Sometimes my tongue feels like lead in my mouth
There are always words I want to say
But they so often become a dead weight in my throat

"Never love a poet"
It's a common warning
"Don't become a muse"

Why is being an inspiration something to dread
Knowing you help create art should be a good thing
Knowing you are the reason behind each paint stroke
The reason behind every word

Why can't that be something beautiful?
Why can't it be something that gives you a sense of pride?

Being a muse means looking at something someone has poured their soul into
And knowing they did it for you

When your head was resting on my chest
You said you could hear my heartbeat
You said it was like thunder

Then you said some cheesy line
Then you wrapped your arms around me

You chuckled and said you could hear it skip a beat

But you don't know that it does that every time you talk
Every time you wrap yourself around me
Every morning we wake up together and you're so quick to kiss me

It takes so little effort for you to weaken my knees
And I wouldn't change it for the world

This poem is for all the eldest daughters
Those who are always the bigger person
Those of us who clench our fists and bite our tongues

We were the ones to watch others
But who was watching us?

While we made meals for others
Who made sure we ate something other than the scraps

While we helped with homework
Who made sure we got ours done before 2 A.M

When we made sure everyone was in bed
Who was left awake to make sure we slept

Eldest daughters are so often overlooked

If you ever ask why I write
I already know what I would say

I write because I need too
I write because I don't know my thoughts until they are written
Sometimes it hurts
Sometimes it simply explains how I feel

Every time it is healing

I have lived long enough to know men
I know their desires

I have been burnt by the flame of what some men call love
I have drowned in falsified affections
I have been pulled apart by their jealousy

Trust is not something I give without cause
My body has been through every flame

I fear no hell from you

I have a tendency to give more than I will ever get

I give more effort
I give more time

I will stretch myself thin
Until I finally tear

Some people are destined to be givers
They always give more love
Then they with ever receive

How badly I wish I wasn't one of them

Maybe it could be considered obsessive
The way I'm almost always thinking about you

I'm worried the words I write will drive you away
I'm scared you'll see every little truth
I'm petrified you'll say I'm too much

Each of these words are pieces of me
Every poem comes from my heart

I'm only trying to be honest with you
My heart has been hidden for a while
I don't want a reason to hide it again

Years ago
A single night tore me apart
A single hour destroyed my world

I'm still haunted by it
No matter how many times I push it away
No matter how deep I bury it

The smells
The feeling
The sounds

I remember everything
And it's slowly killing me inside

I've told the stars about you
The moon knows your name

Mars knows what you mean to me
The Sun knows I burn for you with the same intensity
Venus knows my deepest desires
Saturn has listened to every love-sick ramble
Pluto has read every poem

I've whispered secrets to the galaxy
The universe knows my heart

I love the kisses you give me
Each and every single one sends my heart into a frenzy

The gentle ones
The ones early in the morning
When we're both half awake
The ones you leave on the back of my hands

The hungry ones
Where you trail your hand up my shirt at the same time
When we only pull apart to breathe
The ones that almost always lead to more

The hello kisses
The goodbye kisses
The good morning and goodnight kisses

Each of them makes my heart skip a beat

I've always been a romantic
I was raised by one

My Father taught me what love could be
He showed me by making roses out of cotton and steel
By buying my Mother her favourite chocolate

With rings made from spoons
And glasses of wine after long days

I was taught what love could be
And I've always wanted a love like that

Someone once told me
That I should be seen not heard
At some point that evolved
Now I'm neither seen nor heard

Except by you

You look at me like there's something worth looking for
You listen to me like there's something worth hearing

I know my words won't fall on deaf ears
I know any tears I shed won't be overlooked

I know I'm both seen and heard by you

Sometimes I see things
Things of the past
Things that try as I may
I cannot forget

Some things sound too similar
There are sounds almost identical
To the sound of a car engine being crushed

Some things smell too similar
There are smells almost identical
To the smell of a cold hospital room with my brother on the bed

Some things feel too similar
There are things that feel almost identical
To the feeling of a rough rope on my skin

How pleasing forgetting seems
I wish I could push things down
I wish I could bury them

The past regularly changes the size of its influence

Most of the time
It's as small as a flea
Irritating but easy to ignore

Occasionally
It's a magpie
Refusing to silence its headache-inducing call

Rarely
It's a wolf
Biting at your heels with violent, bone-crushing aggression

The flea, the magpie, and the wolf
They wait patiently to show themselves
Prepare yourself for when they do

The comfort of your breathing lulls me to sleep
It's a smooth rhythm
Accompanied by the steady beat of your heart

It's like a muted symphony
With your hair in my hand
Like you conduct my dreams

The hum of your voice is a low bass
Your laugh is like a cymbal crash
Your hand playing with mine as though you're plucking harp strings

In these little moments
I can hear the music of you

The timing of inspiration is never convenient
It always has to be a distraction

It comes in the middle of conversations
When you're trying to sleep
When you have no way to record it

Inspiration is a fickle thing

It's hard to find in silence
It's never there when you have a pen in your hand

When it does come
By the time you sit down
It's already left

I have received many red roses
Beautiful bouquets begging for forgiveness
But if I look closely at the ruby petals
I notice their shade belongs to blood

The colour red symbolizes so much
Passion, strength, love

But a colour like that can disguise anything
Anger, hate, danger

Sometimes it takes too long to notice
What message you're receiving

To some
It could be seen as an addiction
The way I am constantly thinking about your touch

When we're apart
My hand will trace my lips
My mind will wander

I'll think about where you've kissed me
How your lips felt
I'll think about where your hands touched
How it felt to be held by you

Even when we're together
I just want to get you alone
Just to experience it all again

Lately, I've been noticing more tangles in my life
My hair gets knotted
Necklaces are now tied together

I know the knots in my hair mean I need a haircut
And I need to be more careful with delicate chains

But there are knots I can't undo alone
The ones in my head
They feel like balls of yarn stuck together

But there is a knot I've grown quite fond of
One that I watch become more entangled
It's the one that you've left
Tied around my heart and soul

Sometimes I'll wake up in pain
I'll whisper a prayer out of habit
Offering up my voice to a God I know isn't listening

I'll close my eyes again as pain sweeps through me
Waiting, begging for it to stop
Gripping my bedsheets in my fists

On these painful mornings
It becomes so very clear

Something inside me is broken
Everything inside me is broken

In my grief
I do not sob or wail
It is silent
Yet it is persistent

It is an agitated animal
Pacing its cage

It is an approaching storm
Darkening the sky with its dark clouds

It is pools of blood
Soaking through an unstitched wound

So many ignore it
But I do not blame them
Tears are hard to notice when they fall in silence

When I am old
With white hair and wrinkled skin
And my body is failing
When my hands can't grip yours with the same strength I have now
Know I will still hold you

When I am old
And my mind is no longer my own
When I can no longer put a name to your face
Know I will still call you "love"

And even if I'm not sure why
I will beg the stars to take me first
So that I will not die twice

As a poet
I'm constantly searching for new words

Words to describe the pain
The love
The joy
The sadness
Every feeling under the sun

And while there are words I've found to describe them
No word will ever be beautiful enough
To describe how beautiful you are to me

But I promise you
I will spend the rest of my life
Searching for them

Home is a strange thing to me
I've moved houses too many times
To have one town be where I grew up

I spent my earliest years in a bustling city
Hours spent on my Father's shoulders
I swore I was as tall as the rain-soaked concrete towers

Then we moved to a smaller town
Family was closer now
My brother made it bigger

My family chased a warmer climate
A city soaked in wine and lake water
I grew up too quickly there

Each place means something
Each one took a piece of me
Each one has a fraction of my soul

Sleep Darling
Collapse on my bed
Take my hand in yours
And let me hold you close

Your eyes look heavy
Your movements are sluggish

I know this exhaustion
I know it as well as I know the sound of your voice
Even though with this exhaustion
Your voice is quiet and rough

Sleep Darling
Even though I know
The exhaustion lies not in your body
But your soul

I've always had a name in my family
"The girl in the books"

Which
Given my collection
Probably isn't completely inaccurate

But I was only ever reading
How badly I wished the pages would swallow me up
How I longed to truly be a part of those stories
I wanted nothing more

I was told it was childish to wish for a world
Where everything was prophesized
Where love was a destiny
Where everyone would have a purpose

So, the girl in the books grew up
Now she's the woman writing them

I'm waiting for the day when everything changes

When "It's late, I should go"
Becomes "It's late, come to bed"

When "Come over"
Becomes "Come home"

When "You and me"
Becomes "All of us"

I'll admit I'm not sure what peace should feel like
But recently I think I've started to learn

It's my head in your lap
With your hand in my hair

It's our hands intertwined
And you kiss the back of my hand

It's the warmth of you beside me
Early in the morning with your arms around me

When you touch me like that
I feel a little less war-torn

I want to know how you ended up like this
So good
So kind
So perfect

What author drafted your story
What sculptor moulded your heart

What painter chose the colour of your eyes
What musician composed your voice

I want to know
What team of artists
Made you so right for me

Growing up
I didn't know my Mother's name
My Father only called her sweetheart

I want a love like that

One where names become secondary
We know what they are
But names don't carry enough love for us

So we use nicknames
My love
Darling
Hun

There's more love in those words
Then any name could carry

We were drunk when we confessed
A few drinks too many
A friend shouted some encouragement

You kept falling off the sidewalk
You couldn't walk straight
I had to wrap my arms around you

The walk back to my place was loud
But it was filled with laughter and joy

Even though we stumbled down my stairs
We did it together

A pen and paper are all I need
In order to translate my heart

The translations may be riddles
But they explain exactly what I mean when I go quiet

When spoken words fail
I know the ones I write will shine through
I know they will explain it all

So I hope you understand
What every word means

I enjoy discovering every little thing about you
Each time I find something new
I fall for you more

You listen to love songs from a bygone era
Humming along
Saying how much you love each one

You're so quick to take care of others
Listening to every word they say
Offering advice as they need it

So every new thing I discover
Every new mannerism of yours I learn
Makes me fall in love with you more

I think I'm in love with you
But how do I put it into words?
I could just say "I love you"
But that doesn't do it justice

I am enamoured by your entire being
I am fascinated by your hands
You are an inspiration and a gift
I adore your mind and spirit

You make simple things extraordinary
I could spend hours simply sitting with you
Listening to you talk for hours
As long as you hold me in your arms

Everyone's life is a book
Most are unfinished
Some are cut short

My book is average
Things go as predicted
I'm rarely surprised by the next chapter

But you
You were a plot twist
I turned the page
And you were unexpectedly there

I hope when I get to the last page
It's marked with "You and I"

There are some people I need to speak around
Silence feels wrong around them
Like it presses down on everyone's bones

Without words
I can't understand what those people are thinking
There is no communication

But you and I
We don't need the constant flow of words
I love how our hearts understand each other
Even in silence

My thoughts are prone to wander
Usually, they wander to important things
Tasks I need to complete

But sometimes my thoughts wander
They wander right into your arms
Right beside you
Where I long to be

Sometimes I wonder
If when your thoughts wander
They wander toward me
The same way mine do

I could tell you were tired last night
When you came through my door
And your voice was hoarse
Any you only held me tight

We stood like that for a while
Your one hand playing with my hair
Your head resting on top of mine

I listened to your heartbeat
I felt your breathing
The tension in your body eased
I only hope any stress in your mind did too

I have a set of rules for myself
Things I prayed I will never forget
These rules kept me safe

Never show how much pain you're really in
Hint at it
But hide how much it truly hurts

Don't fall in love too quickly
Don't forbid it
But do not jump the cliff without knowing the depth of the water

Don't rely too much on others
Lean on people
But don't let them be a crutch

I've started breaking my rules for you

From what I've seen
Everyone has a person

Someone that fits them so well
Someone who knows them better than anyone
Someone that they go to for comfort
Someone that they share every success with

To me
You're it
You're my person

I don't believe in accidents
Everything was designed to happen

Leaves don't accidentally change from green to red
The sun doesn't accidentally shine
Snow and rain don't accidentally fall
Flowers don't accidentally grow

It's no accident how well my hand fits in yours
It's no accident I feel so in love with you
Souls don't meet accidentally

I often catch myself counting
Keeping track of things

I count the hours until I can see you again
I count how many mornings I wake up in your arms
I count the days I've been calling you mine

I can't wait for the day I can stop counting

Because I'll know I'll see you at the end of the day
Because I'll know I'll always wake up beside you
Because I'll know I'll have the rest of my life to call you mine

Even though I know you won't react poorly
I know there will be no anger
I'm still afraid to say every word that's begging for release

Like how I like getting flowers
Wisteria's my favourite
It symbolizes love, creativity, patience and honour

How I would love to steal your t-shirts
I'd wear them constantly
Just to feel a little closer to you in your absence

Give me a bag with a dress inside
Tell me to be ready by seven
And take me out for an evening

When we return home
Kiss me the way you do
Pull me to bed
And let me fall asleep in your arms

My favourite colour has often changed
From pink, to blue, to yellow
It's finally settled on green

But only specific shades
The shade of leaves in the middle of summer
Moss or ivy growing on stone

The shades have always been deep
Dark
Moody

But recently there's been a new shade
A shade so unique
I can only find it in one place

That place is you
When I look into your eyes
I'm met with the most beautiful green I've ever seen

My dear brother
I've written many poems
And this one's for you

Though I know I haven't always been perfect
Know that no matter what
Your big sister is here for you

I wish you strength and luck
I wish you peace and love
In all your endeavours
I wish you success

Know that no matter where you are
I am thinking of you
And I am so proud

I am honoured to call you my brother

Dear Mom

I know we have our fights
We argue
We stop talking for a while

And maybe we're both too stubborn
Maybe I'm just I little too much like you to say it
I know I don't say it enough

But I am thankful for you
You've always been there
Everything you've done
Every sacrifice you make

I love you for it
You taught me how to be strong

Dear Dad

In all your chaos
In your weirdness
I find myself

I am never ashamed of myself
Because you taught me weird is good
Because you wear your heart on your sleeve
And taught me to do the same

You taught me how to enjoy life
And I will keep enjoying it
Every little challenge and success
Just like you taught me

Thank you
For being the best teacher
A little girl could ask for

I like to plan things out
Writing itineraries for daily use
Planning my days out months in advance

I've planned my whole life out
Of course, I'm aware plans change
So, I never set them in stone
They simply exist

I must have forgotten
That some things can't be planned

Which is why I shouldn't have been surprised
When I fell in love with you
Faster and harder than I planned

I like to think I don't fear much
But I know there are deep-rooted fears inside me

I am afraid of ladders
I hate being on top of them
My fear makes me shake
Which makes the ladder shake

I'm not afraid of the dark
Just the things that hide in it
Alone outside at night
I fear something is watching me

My deepest fear
What truly wakes me from sleep
What stops my heart when I think of it
Is losing you

Everyone knows that time is finite
That one day it will all end

One day we will lose
Every star
Every galaxy
Every sun

One day
Every light will go out
Every sound will quiet
Every heart will stop

Know even then
Even then I will be yours

I have a hard time letting things go
I will hold on to things longer than needed
Often until someone has to take it from me
Or it leaves because of its own volition

Sometimes it's people
And I understand why
We drift apart
We stop talking

Sometimes it's actual objects
And it's usually my fault
They break
They get lost

But I am asking
Begging
For you to let me keep you

I've always loved art
Creating it
Viewing it
As long as I was surrounded by it

I judged books by the art on their cover
Patterns and colours
They distract me
I could stare at them for hours

You are art
I could stare at endlessly

I'll be the first to admit
My memory isn't that great
But there are things I refuse to forget

The feeling of the ocean on my skin
The way a summer at a lake smells
The taste of smooth wine
The sight of the mountain woods
The sound of my favourite song

So, I pray
To any deity listening
That I will never forget you

One hundred poems
One hundred feelings
Seven thousand words

I've seen grief
Anger
Love
Joy
Longing

I thank my heart for feeling so much
I thank my mind for having the words to explain it
I thank my life for being so full.

CPSIA information can be obtained
at www.ICGtesting.com
Printed in the USA
LVHW100740260323
742232LV00001B/3